The Stars Also Shine

Erin Sledge

The Stars Also Shine © 2022 Erin Sledge

All rights reserved.

No part of this publication may be reproduced, stored in a retrieval system, or transmitted, in any form or by any means, electronic, mechanical, photocopying, recording or otherwise, without the prior written permission of the presenters.

Erin Sledge asserts the moral right to be identified as author of this work.

Presentation by *BookLeaf Publishing*

Web: www.bookleafpub.com

E-mail: info@bookleafpub.com

ISBN : 9789394788077

First edition 2022

ACKNOWLEDGEMENT

Mom and dad, I am infinitely grateful for your support throughout the years. I wouldn't be the person that I am today without you. I know it wasn't always easy, but you always encouraged me to follow my dreams and find something that I loved. Emily, thank you for always supporting me in everything that I do. Even when it took me far away, you always made sure that I knew you were there for me.

Light

I didn't realize
how much your light
brightened my life
until it went out.

Loss

The people who
burn the brightest
always seem to disappear
Like they've gone home
to join the other stars.

Purpose

I think
It is better
to live a bright life
that touches many
than a long life
that touches few
So that once you're gone
the people you touched
may remember your light.

Exist

There are days
when knowing
that you're out there
existing
is enough.

Love

I looked at you
and I fell
like Icarus
who flew too close
to the sun.

Thief

I want to open myself up
to you
But I know
you would take
everything
and leave me
an empty shell.

Caught

You found me
a little bird
with a broken wing
but instead of helping me
you broke the other,
and said you much prefer it
when I cannot fly.

Abyss

Sometimes
it feels like
there's a hole
where your heart should be
And if I look too close
I might fall in.

Neglect

Even a silver spoon
will tarnish and decay
as time passes
if it is not properly
taken care of.

If you can't even
take care of
a spoon,
where does that
leave me?

Ungrateful

I could lay the world
at your feet
and you would say
"I wanted the moon".

Growth

It feels like
the world must stop
when you close your eyes
But then I open mine
and realize
my life goes on.

Value

I was happy
when you picked me
but then I realized
you wouldn't stay
And I needed
to choose myself.

Stars

You were my Sun
but the stars also shine
and maybe it's time
to learn to live
by the moon.

Confidence

She had grace
and poise
but she moved
like a natural disaster
She destroyed
and she created
And to see her was to think
that wherever she went
the stars surely followed.

Adult

Does growing up
mean being
less afraid
of the dark
Or learning how
to go to sleep
anyway?

Reality

Being an adult
doesn't mean having
grand dreams
or big accomplishments.

Sometimes
it's just wishing
for a job that doesn't
give you nightmares.

Anxious

Anxiety is
the thoughts in the night
that keep you from sleep
And the dreams
that make you wish
you had stayed awake.

Gravity

I want to be
the type of person
that people gravitate to.

I want to have
my own pull
if only to make sure
I won't ever
be alone.

Bored

The world
is a little monotonous
as an adult.

Like all the color
was sucked out of it
when I started my
nine-to-five.

It makes it hard to exist
for someone
who likes to live
in color.

Calling

I'm not sure I have a calling
to be completely honest.
I've never known
what I wanted to do
or who I wanted to be
But if all else fails
I know I like
to write.

Future

The future feels
a little less bright
without you in it.

But in the end
I know
I will persist.

Printed in the USA
CPSIA information can be obtained
at www.ICGtesting.com
LVHW011705280723
753396LV00019B/1569

9 789394 788077